MY FIRST BOOK

RUSSIA

ALL ABOUT RUSSIA FOR KIDS

GL🌐BED
CHILDREN BOOKS

Interior and cover Design: Daniel Day

Editor: Margaret Bam

For My Sons, Daniel, David and Jude

Saint Basil's Cathedral, Russia

Russia

Russia is a **country**.

A country is land that is controlled by a **single government**. Countries are also called **nations, states, or nation-states**.

Countries can be **different sizes**. Some countries are big and others are small.

Hotel Ukraina, Moscow, Russia

Where Is Russia?

Russia is located in the continent of **Europe**.

A continent is **a massive area of land that is separated from others by water or other natural features**.

Russia is situated in the eastern part of Europe.

St. Basil Cathedral, Red Square, Moscow

Capital

The capital of Russia is Moscow.

Moscow is located in the **western part** of the country.

Moscow is the largest city in Russia.

St. Petersburg, Russia

Territories

Russia is a country that is made up of 21 territories.

The territories of Russia are as follows:

Adygea, Altai, Bashkortostan, Buryatia, Dagestan Ingushetia, Kabardino-Balkaria, Kalmykia, Karachay-Cherkessia, Karelia, Komi, Mari El, Mordovia, Sakha, North Ossetia–Alania, Tatarstan, Tuva, Udmurtia, Khakassia, Chechnya and Chuvashia.

Soldiers marching during St Petersburg parade

Population

Russia has population of around **143 million people** making it the 9th most populated country in the world and the most populated country in Europe.

Size

Russia is **17,098,242 square kilometres** making it the largest country in Europe by area.

Russia is the largest country in the world.

Languages

The official language of Russia is **Russian**. The Russian language originated in Russia and is now spoken by hundreds of millions of people across the world.

Russian is the world's eighth most spoken language.

Here are a few Russian phrases
- **Доброе утро** - Good morning
- **Как дела?** - How are you?

Catherine Palace in Pushkin

Attractions

There are lots of interesting places to see in Russia.

Some beautiful places to visit in Russia are

- State Hermitage Museum
- The Moscow Kremlin
- St. Basil's Cathedral
- Red Square
- Peterhof
- The Pushkin State Museum of Fine Arts

Peterhof Palace, Russia

History of Russia

People have lived in Russia for a very long time. In fact, it is believed that the first trace of an early modern human in Russia dates back to 45,000 years, in Western Siberia.

On 30th December 1922, Lenin and his aides formed the Soviet Union, joining the Russian SFSR into a single state with the Byelorussian, Transcaucasian, and Ukrainian republics. The Soviet Union was dissolved on 26 December 1991.

A woman in traditional Russian dress

Customs in Russia

Russia has many fascinating customs and traditions.

- **Christmas is a very popular celebration in Russia. Some Russians celebrate Christmas on January 7 in accordance to the Julian calendar. It is also common to see Santa Claus wearing blue instead of red.**
- **Family is very important to Russian people, and each family is dependent upon all its members. Usually, families in Russia are large and many generations can live together under the same roof.**

St Basil's Cathedral

Music of Russia

There are many different music genres in Russia such as **Russian folk music, Russian hip hop, Russian chanson, Russian pop, Bard and Russian rock.**

Some notable Russian musicians include
- **Tatiana Aleshina**
- **Regina Spektor**
- **Dima Bilan**
- **Pyotr Ilyich Tchaikovsky**
- **Sergey Shnurov**

Pelmeni

Food of Russia

Russia is known for having delicious, flavoursome and rich dishes.

The national dish of Russia is **Pelmeni** which is a pastry dumpling filled with minced meat.

Food of Russia

Some popular dishes in Russia include

- **Beef Stroganoff**
- **Syrniki**
- **Kasha (Porridge)**
- **Borscht**
- **Okroshka**

Seaport in Sochi, Russia

Weather in Russia

Russia is a very big country which means it has a varied climate.

Russia's climate ranges from steppes in the south, humid continental in the European parts of Russia, subarctic in Siberia to a tundra climate in the polar north.

Siberian tiger in Russia

Animals of Russia

There are many wonderful animals in Russia.

Here are some animals that live in Russia

- Siberian tiger
- Brown bear
- Edible dormouse
- Grey wolf
- Northern fur seal
- Polar bear
- Common northern viper

Magadan beach, Russia

Beaches

There are many beautiful beaches in Russia which is one of the reasons why so many people visit this beautiful country every year.

Here are some of Russia's beaches

- Beach Promenade
- Khalaktyrsky Beach
- Astafyev's Bay
- Beach Yagrinskiy
- Golden Beach

Russian football fan

Sports of Russia

Sports play an integral part in Russian culture. The most popular sport is **Football.**

Here are some of famous sportspeople from Russia

- **Igor Akinfeev - Football**
- **Fyodor Smolov - Football**
- **Artem Dzyuba - Football**
- **Vasily Artemyev - Rugby**

Kremlin, Moscow, Russia

Famous

Many successful people hail from Russia.

Here are some notable Russian figures

- **Vladimir Putin – Politician**
- **Mikhail Gorbachev – Politician**
- **Alexander Ovechkin – Ice Hockey Player**
- **Aleksandr Solzhenitsyn – Novelist**
- **Roman Abramovich – Football club owner**

Sergiev Posad Monastery

Something Extra...

As a little something extra, we are going to share some lesser known facts about Russia.

- Russia is home to the world's longest railway.
- There are 12 Active Volcanos in Russia.
- The game 'Tetris' was invented in Russia.

Words From the Author

We hope that you enjoyed learning about the wonderful country of Russia.

Russia is a country rich in culture and beauty, with lots of wonderful places to visit and people to meet.

We hope you continue to learn more about this wonderful nation. If you enjoyed this book, consider leaving a review!

With Love